Cornerstones of Freedom

Lexington and Concord

Deborah Kent

CHILDREN'S PRESS®
A Division of Grolier Publishing
New York • London • Hong Kong • Sydney
Danbury, Connecticut

Library of Congress Cataloging-in-Publication Data

Kent, Deborah.
  Lexington and Concord / Deborah Kent
    p. cm.—(Cornerstones of freedom)
  Includes index.
  Summary: Describes the first battles of the Revolutionary War,
the events leading up to the conflict, and the effect of helping the
thirteen British colonies pull together for a common cause.
  ISBN 0-516-20462-9 (lib.bdg) 0-516-26229-7 (pbk.)
  1. Lexington, Battle of, 1775—Juvenile literature. 2. Concord,
Battle of, 1775—Juvenile literature. [1. Lexington, Battle of, 1775.
2. Concord, Battle of, 1775. 3. United States—History—Revolution,
1775–1783—Campaigns.] I. Title. II. Series.
E241.L6K46 1997
973.3'311—dc21
                                                                97-3438
                                                                   CIP
                                                                    AC

The night of April 18, 1775, was chilly and clear. From a pier in the village of Charlestown, a silent watchman gazed across the Charles River toward the city of Boston. Suddenly two tiny lights shone over the water. They gleamed from the steeple of Boston's North Church. The watchman strained to be certain. Yes, two lanterns glowed, sending forth a special message.

The watchman belonged to a secret organization called the Massachusetts Committee of Safety. The Committee of Safety was a network of colonial spies that gathered information about British plans and activities. The spies had learned that the British intended to send troops from Boston to the nearby towns of Lexington and Concord. The lanterns in the church steeple were a prearranged signal. If the watchman saw one light, he would know that the British were moving out of Boston by land. Two lights meant that the troops would row across the Charles River instead.

One of the signal lanterns

The watchman waited for a prearranged signal from Boston's North Church, just visible on the horizon.

Furious colonists burn stamps to protest British taxes.

For ten years, tension had mounted between Great Britain and its thirteen colonies in North America. In 1765, England attempted to raise much-needed revenue by levying new taxes on the colonies. The colonists had no representatives in the British Parliament. They were furious over the taxes, and many refused to pay. Fiery colonial orators proclaimed that "taxation without representation is tyranny."

Parliament passed one new tax after another. Massachusetts led the colonies in vigorous protest. It launched a boycott of tea and other imported British goods. The boycott spread to many of the other colonies. In the past, the colonies had seen themselves as very separate entities. They felt bound to Great Britain but not to one another. Now a new sense of unity began to grow among the colonies.

To punish the rebels in Massachusetts, the British blockaded Boston Harbor. No trading

British stamps

In response to colonial protest, British soldiers entered Boston.

vessels could sail in or out. British troops under General Thomas Gage occupied the city. Red-coated British soldiers patrolled Boston's streets.

The British regarded the colonial rebels with contempt. One British officer wrote that the Americans were "the most absolute cowards on the face of the earth." Firmness and a bit of force would restore order. In March 1775, a British official in Massachusetts proclaimed, "I'm satisfied that one active campaign, a smart action and burning two or three of their towns, will set everything to rights."

General Thomas Gage

The presence of British troops outraged the people of Massachusetts. Yet most still hoped to be reconciled with the mother country. The colonies had been tied to Great Britain for more than 150 years. In 1775, few colonists imagined severing that bond to form an independent nation.

If necessary, however, the colonists felt they must meet force with force. Most towns and villages already maintained bands of soldiers called militia. Now many communities began to train additional volunteer forces. These volunteers

A colonial minuteman

were known as minutemen because they were prepared to fight at a minute's notice.

Like the colonists, the British maintained a network of spies. Early in April 1775, General Gage learned that the colonists had stored weapons and other supplies in Concord. He also discovered that two of the most active rebel leaders, Samuel Adams and John Hancock, were hiding in Lexington. Gage decided to send troops on a mission to the two villages. The British would destroy the supplies and capture the rebel ringleaders. Perhaps the successful completion of this mission would finally bring the trouble in Massachusetts to an end.

Samuel Adams (left) and John Hancock (right) enthusiastically called for the defense of American liberty.

During the night of April 18, the British soldiers assembled and prepared to march. Two colonial couriers on horseback, however, already galloped toward Lexington and Concord. They were under orders to warn everyone along the way about the British advance. The couriers were named William Dawes and Paul Revere.

Nearly one hundred years later, the poet Henry Wadsworth Longfellow wrote a poem about this historic night. Generations of girls and boys learned to recite its opening lines: "Listen, my children, and you shall hear, Of the midnight ride of Paul Revere . . ." Today, most Americans know about Paul Revere's famous ride, but William Dawes's name has nearly been lost in history. The name Revere rhymes more easily than the name Dawes. Through the craft of a poet, one man became a legend, while the other was almost forgotten.

Even without Longfellow's aid, Paul Revere would hold a place in American lore. A skilled silversmith and engraver, he was a close friend of John Hancock, Samuel Adams, John Adams, and many other Massachusetts patriots. In December 1773, Revere dressed as a Mohawk Indian and joined a band of protesters as they dumped chests of British tea into Boston Harbor. The incident is remembered as the Boston Tea Party.

Both before the Revolution and during it, Paul Revere made enormous contributions to the American cause.

Paul Revere rode through the countryside, alerting the minutemen to the British advance.

Revere had scarcely left Charlestown when two British officers spotted him on the road. Suspecting that he was a rebel messenger, the officers gave chase. As Revere later explained, he rode "a very good horse." Leaping stone walls and racing across fields and pastures,

he escaped his pursuers. Here and there on his 18-mile (29-km) journey to Lexington, he stopped to wake farmers, blacksmiths, and tradesmen. "The British are coming!" he called. Revere spread the alarm at isolated farmhouses and in crowded towns. Sleepy patriots scrambled out of bed and grabbed their muskets. Militia units began to assemble and prepare for action.

Frantic minutemen scrambled from their beds after hearing Paul Revere's news.

The British soldier, called a "Regular," was well-trained and brave in battle.

In Lexington, John Hancock and Samuel Adams were staying at the home of Reverend Jonas Clark. The house was surrounded by armed militiamen. When Revere rode up, the guards told him to halt. Later one of them recalled, "I told [Revere] the family had just retired, and had requested that they might not be disturbed by any noise about the house. 'Noise!' he said. 'You'll have noise enough before long! The Regulars are coming out!'"

When the guards let him pass, Revere woke Adams and Hancock. As he was telling them his story, William Dawes arrived. The two messengers persuaded Adams and Hancock to flee to safety. After resting for half an hour, the couriers set off once more, heading on to Concord.

At 2:00 A.M. on the morning of April 19, a church bell tolled over Lexington. Its somber chime called the militia to the village green. About seventy militiamen gathered with their elected leader, Captain John Parker. Restlessly they listened for the tramp of marching boots and the jingle of harnesses. But the British failed to arrive. After two hours of waiting, Captain Parker told the militia to disperse. Many of the men went home to get some sleep. The rest made for a nearby tavern. Captain Parker told the men to reassemble as soon as they heard a drum beat the call to arms. The night's work was not yet over.

On Lexington Green, the minutemen formed a line and waited for the British troops.

The British had made a slow start. They left Boston at about 10:00 P.M. in boats with muffled oars, hoping to conceal their movements from the colonists. Crossing the Charles River, they landed on Cambridge Marsh. There they were ordered to halt. Knee-deep in water and mud, the men waited more than two hours for provisions. At last the supplies were hauled from the boats and divided among the troops. The provisions that caused the long delay were not even needed. Most of the men had brought food for the march, and they threw the new supplies away.

From Boston, the British rowed north across the Charles River to Cambridge. From there, they marched north toward Lexington.

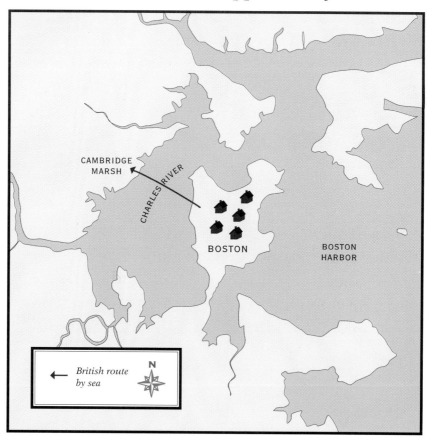

As the first light of dawn streaked the sky, the heavy beat of a drum sounded through Lexington. Again, militiamen scrambled from their beds and fumbled for their muskets. More men rushed in confusion from the tavern. Suddenly, some of the troops realized that they had no ammunition. They stormed into the town meetinghouse, where powder and musket balls were stored.

Finally the militia assembled once more on Lexington Green, an open grassy triangle in the middle of the town. Captain Parker did not expect a battle to erupt. Never in his experience had British soldiers fired upon Americans, people who were British subjects themselves. Now that Samuel Adams and John Hancock were gone, the British had no reason to linger in Lexington. Perhaps they would simply turn and march back to Boston. "Don't fire unless fired upon," Parker told his men. "But if they want a war, let it begin here."

Shortly after 5:00 A.M., six hundred British troops under Colonel Francis Smith and Major John Pitcairn marched into Lexington. The sun shone on their scarlet coats and glinted off their rifle barrels and bayonets. They outnumbered the militia by nearly ten to one. Seeing that overwhelming odds were against them, Captain Parker ordered the militia to disperse. The men began to scatter as the British columns approached.

Major John Pitcairn

15

No one will ever be certain who fired the first shot on Lexington Green. In the years that followed, most British eyewitnesses told one story, while the Americans generally had a different version. One of the observers was Reverend Jonas Clark, the Lexington pastor who hid Samuel Adams and John Hancock in his home. According to Clark's account, Colonel Smith, Major Pitcairn, or a third officer "advanced on horseback to the front of the body, and coming within five or six rods of the militia, one of them cried out, 'You villains, you rebels, disperse! Damn you, disperse!'" Another officer fired his pistol toward the militia. The third officer brandished his sword, shouting, "Fire! By God, fire!" and a volley of shots burst from the British ranks. But Colonel Smith, the commanding British officer, claimed that the militia fired first. In a letter following the battle he wrote, "They [the militia] in confusion went off, . . . only one of them fired before he went, and three or four more jumped over a wall and fired from behind it among the soldiers."

Within moments, guns blazed from both sides. The militia fired from behind trees and fences while the British bombarded them with one heavy volley after another. Major Pitcairn rode back and forth among his troops, frantically ordering them to stop. But he had lost control of the soldiers. As one officer

explained later, "The men were so wild they could hear no orders."

At last, amid the noise and bloodshed, Colonel Smith called for a drummer boy. He ordered the drummer to sound the signal for cease-fire. The drumbeats finally reached the frenzied men, and they put down their arms. Eight Americans lay dead, and fourteen more were wounded. The British, who had suffered no casualties, gave three cheers of triumph.

The American militia scattered in the face of superior British numbers and firepower.

After the battle on Lexington Green, most of the British officers wanted to return to Boston. They had not captured Adams and Hancock, but the rebels were soundly routed. Now, however, tales of British atrocities would leap from one farmhouse to the next. The surrounding countryside would be roused to arms, and the British would be in serious danger. Surely nothing could be gained by pushing on toward Concord.

Colonel Smith would not give in to argument. "I have my orders," he insisted. "I am determined to obey them." Reluctantly, the British marched toward Concord as they had planned from the beginning.

Like the people of Lexington, the citizens of Concord knew that the British were on their way. Paul Revere was captured by British soldiers soon after he galloped out of Lexington. Another messenger, Dr. Samuel Prescott, reached Concord by 2:30 A.M. Rumors of British movements had been flying for the past ten days. Concord farmers buried cannons and balls in their newly plowed fields, and they hid muskets under piles of manure. Guns, balls, and powder were also concealed in more than a dozen homes.

Drums beat and bugles sounded, mustering six companies of militia and minutemen (about 250 troops) from Concord and several neighboring villages. Inflamed by the story of Lexington, the men thirsted for vengeance. But when the British Regulars swept into view, militia commander Colonel James Barrett made a swift decision. Instead of trying to hold Concord, he moved his men to a ridge north of the town. The militia watched in anguish as the British poured through the streets, looting and burning one home after another.

This painting by James Earl depicts the British soldiers marching into Concord.

A flag carried by the militia at the North Bridge.

At the North Bridge, American militia and British Regulars meet in battle.

The militia finally met the British face to face across Concord's North Bridge. Once more muskets thundered, and smoke filled the air. Two militia men and three British soldiers were killed, and many more were wounded. Shocked by the rebels' bold stand, the British withdrew in confusion. Colonel Smith commandeered carriages and wagons to transport his injured men. At last he re-formed the columns and began the long march back to Boston. "The British marched down the hill with slow but steady steps," wrote a militia private, "without music or a word being spoken that could be heard. Silence reigned on both sides."

The silence did not last long. All along the road from Concord, militiamen crouched behind trees and stone walls, their muskets at the ready. Armed farmers watched from their windows, waiting to pick off soldiers as they passed. As soon as the British columns left Concord, snipers began to pepper them with shots. "The country was an amazing strong one, full of hills, woods, stone walls, etc., which the rebels did not fail to take advantage of," recalled one British officer. "[The roads] were all lined with people who kept an incessant fire upon us. . . . They were so concealed there was hardly any seeing them. In this way we marched between nine and ten miles, their numbers increasing from all parts, while ours were reduced by deaths, wounds, and fatigue; and we were totally surrounded with such an incessant fire as it is impossible to conceive."

Still fighting a rearguard action, the British retreat out of Concord.

All along the road back to Boston, the militia used the cover of trees, stone walls, and houses, to shoot at the British column.

The British fired back at random. Since they seldom glimpsed the enemy, their shots had little effect. One British officer wrote in his diary, "The soldiers were so enraged at suffering from an unseen enemy that they forced open many of the houses from which the fire proceeded and put to death all those found in them. Those houses would certainly have been burnt had any fire been found in them, or had there been time to kindle any; but only three or four near where we first formed suffered in this way."

In the town of Menotomy (present-day Somerville) eighty-year-old Samuel Whittemore challenged the oncoming troops from behind a stone wall. "I will not leave," he told them. "I will be willing to die if I can kill one redcoat."

Whittemore actually killed two soldiers, one with his musket and another with his pistol. A British ball finally shattered his cheekbone. Several troops leaped the wall and stabbed him with their bayonets to finish him off. Miraculously, however, the old man survived his dreadful wounds. He lived for another eighteen years, a legend throughout the countryside. "I should do just so again," he said near the close of his long life. "I would run the same chance again."

As the march progressed, the British suffered more casualties.

On Lexington Green the British had cheered in triumph. Now, on the march from Concord, they fled for their lives. Somehow the ragtag Americans, those "most absolute cowards on the face of the earth," had secured the upper hand. The British victory of a few hours before had turned to disaster.

Suddenly, far down the road, Colonel Smith's advance guards saw the dust of an approaching column. Reinforcements marched to greet them, fresh troops under Lord Hugh Percy. Once again the Regulars gave three wild cheers. This time they did not lift their voices in triumph. They cheered because rescue had come at last.

The timely arrival of Lord Hugh Percy with fresh troops saved the British force from complete destruction.

Percy's arrival gave the British a lifesaving surge of morale, even though the snipers continued to harass them. Percy reorganized the tattered columns and led the exhausted men the rest of the way back to their camps in Boston. General Gage praised Percy as the hero of the day. The British lost some 250 men on their long march home, but without Percy's aid the death toll might have been far higher. Percy later extolled the Regulars for their "intrepidity of spirit." The colonists, he claimed, displayed unimaginable cruelty, "scalping and cutting off the ears of some of the wounded men who fell into their hands."

This map shows the great distance the British soldiers marched on April 19.

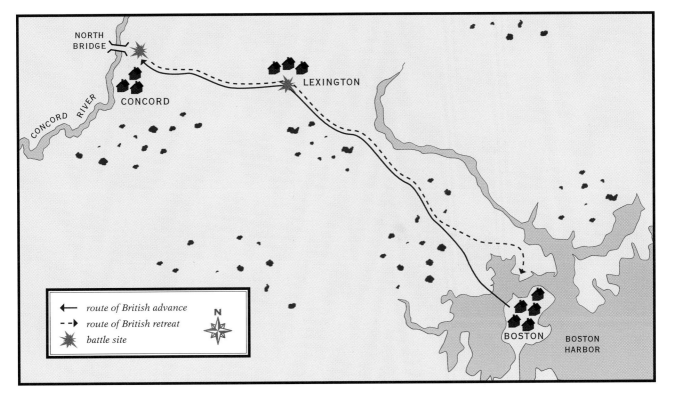

NORTH BRIDGE

CONCORD RIVER

CONCORD

LEXINGTON

route of British advance
route of British retreat
battle site

N

BOSTON

BOSTON HARBOR

The tensions of a decade exploded into violence at the battle of Lexington and Concord. By taking the offensive on Lexington Green, the British gave colonial radicals the very focus they needed. How could the people of Massachusetts endure such an outrage? No longer could they offer peaceful protests, dumping chests of tea into the harbor. Armies had confronted one another. Blood had been shed. The time had come for war.

As he fled from his hiding place in Lexington, Samuel Adams heard the distant rattle of gunfire from the green. He rejoiced that the colonists were finally taking a stand for freedom. "What a

American patriot John Adams

glorious morning for America!" he exclaimed. To this day, his words appear on the seal of the town of Lexington.

Samuel Adams's cousin John Adams, a patriot from Boston, took a more sober view of the day's events. When the fighting was over he wrote, "Yesterday produced a scene the most shocking New England ever beheld. . . . When I reflect and consider that the fight

News of the battle spread quickly through the thirteen colonies.

was between those whose parents but a few generations ago were brothers, I shudder at the thought; and there is no knowing where our calamities will end."

Only hours after the smoke cleared at Concord Bridge, a courier named Israel Bissel set out from Boston. The Massachusetts Committee of Safety sent Bissel to spread the news about the battles. When Bissel reached Worcester, Massachusetts, his exhausted horse dropped dead beneath him. With only a few minutes of rest, Bissel set off again on a fresh mount. The next morning he shared his story with colonial leaders in Connecticut. On April 23, he reached New York City. The following day he spoke to the people of Philadelphia. From all over the colonies, volunteers flocked to Massachusetts to join the growing rebel army. Even the faraway colony of Georgia sent a shipment of rice for the hungry troops.

The Battle of Lexington and Concord helped the thirteen British colonies pull together for a common cause. The following year, on July 4, 1776, the colonies declared their independence from Great Britain. After a long and bloody war, they finally won their freedom.

In modern Concord, Massachusetts (right and opposite), people reenact the battle of Lexington and Concord every year to celebrate the bravery of the minutemen.

On July 4, 1837, a crowd gathered to unveil the Battle Monument in Concord. The poet and philosopher Ralph Waldo Emerson wrote a hymn which was sung at the dedication ceremony. Emerson's words conveyed the impact of the battle that launched America's War of Independence.

By the rude bridge that arched the flood,
Their flag to April's breeze unfurled,
Here once the embattled farmers stood,
And fired the shot heard round the world.

GLOSSARY

atrocity – cruel, bloody deed

commandeer – lay claim to for a military purpose

courier – swift messenger

courier

delegate – representative who has the power to vote

entity – distinct unit

muffle – deaden a sound

orator – skilled public speaker

parliament – lawmaking body

reconcile – resolve differences between persons or groups

revenue – income for a government or an organization

rod – unit of measure equal to $16\,2/3$ feet (5 meters)

British stamp

Stamp Act – British tax put on all paper goods in the colonies

sniper – person who fires shots from a hidden location

tyranny – dominance based on overwhelming power

TIMELINE

1620 Plymouth Colony established
in Massachusetts

Parliament
in London
passes
Stamp Act

Stamp Act is repealed **1766**

1765

1770 Boston Massacre

1773 Boston Tea Party

1775

July 4: Declaration of Independence signed **1776**

United States Constitution signed **1787**

Battle Monument is dedicated at Concord **1837**

Longfellow's "Paul Revere's Ride"
is published **1863**

Massachusetts
designates
April 19 as
Patriot's Day **1894**

April 16:
British plan to
raid Lexington
and Concord

April 18:
Paul Revere and
William Dawes
warn the
minutemen

April 19:
Battle at
Lexington Green
and Concord

INDEX (*Boldface* page numbers indicate illustrations.)

PHOTO CREDITS

©: Concord Museum: 3 top; Corbis–Bettmann: 1, 9, 15, 19, 26, 27; James P. Rowan: 2; New England Stock Photo: 29 (Thomas H. Mitchell); North Wind Picture Archives: cover, 3 bottom, 4, 5, 7, 11, 12, 13, 17, 20, 21, 22, 23, 30 bottom, 31 top left, 31 right; Stock Montage, Inc.: 6, 24; Superstock, Inc.: 10, 28, 30 top, 31 bottom left.

Maps by TJS Design

ABOUT THE AUTHOR

Deborah Kent grew up in Little Falls, New Jersey, and received her B.A. from Oberlin College. She earned a master's degree in social work from Smith College, and worked for four years at the University Settlement House on New York's Lower East Side. University Settlement, though less well-known, actually predates Hull House by two years.

Ms. Kent left social work to begin a career in writing. She published her first novel, *Belonging,* while living in San Miguel de Allende, Mexico. She has written a dozen novels for young adults, as well as numerous nonfiction titles for children. She lives in Chicago with her husband and their daughter Janna.